THE
Most Important
Thing I've Learned
in Life

A Collection of Quotations compiled by BEAU BAUMAN

FIRESIDE BOOKS

SIMON & SCHUSTER / *New York* / *London* / *Toronto* / *Sydney* / *Tokyo* / *Singapore*

FIRESIDE
Rockefeller Center
1230 Avenue of the Americas
New York, New York 10020

Copyright © 1994 by Beau Bauman

FIRESIDE and colophon are registered trademarks of
Simon & Schuster Inc.

Book design by Chris Welch

Manufactured in the United States of America

1 3 5 7 9 10 8 6 4 2

Library of Congress Cataloging-in-Publication Data

The Most Important Thing I've Learned in Life:
a collection of quotations / compiled by Beau Bauman.
p.   cm.
"Fireside book."
1. Life—Quotations, maxims, etc. 2. Conduct of life—Quotations,
maxims, etc.   I. Bauman, Beau.
PN6084.L53M67   1994   94-1278
818' .502080355--dc20   CIP

ISBN: 0-671-89228-2

ACKNOWLEDGMENTS

Very, very, very special thanks to my mother, my inspiration whose always passionate spirit made the difference; my father, a constant source of experienced encouragement—I love you both. And to my agent, Joan Stewart, who guided me through the process of attaining my goal; my editor, Betsy Radin, who shared my enthusiasm about the success of this project; June Giuliani, the most reliable typist in the world; Dan Rattiner for his timely praise; all my other friends and family whose assistance and advice made the book the best it could be; and all of the people who answered my question: to whom I am perhaps most grateful.

THE

Most Important Thing I've Learned in Life

A COLLECTION OF QUOTATIONS
COMPILED BY BEAU BAUMAN

October 1, 1993

Dear

I am a sixteen-year-old boy with a sincere curiosity about life. A particular interest which has resulted from this is a desire to hear and study some of the higher thoughts of human expression.

My idea is to collect and compile the answers of as many people as possible to the question regarding the most important thing they've learned in life. From this I hope to gather enough information to write a book of quotations for publication. I have been working on this project since I was thirteen. I would greatly appreciate your cooperation in helping to achieve this goal by submitting a summary of the most important thing you've learned in life. Because of your experience in life I expect your contribution to be noteworthy. Please respond below.

Thank you.

Yours truly,
Beau Bauman

INTRODUCTION

What is the most important thing you've learned in life? Odds are you probably haven't given it much thought. In fact, neither did I until a little more than a year ago when my mother was listing the most important things she has learned in life. In the typical way a teenage boy speaks to his mother when she's lecturing him, I said, "Mom, why don't you write a book about it." Of course, she then replied, "Oh, why don't you write the book."

I don't know why, but I took her seriously. The details of how to begin the process were quickly filled in. I would compile and edit a book of quotations. I would ask interesting people of different ages, from all different walks of life, what was the most important thing they had learned in life. I would ask writers, professors, actors, doctors, athletes, religious figures, and so on. I was basically looking for people who were successful in what they did. I found an incredible number of addresses in various Who's Who–type publications, fan club directories, and celebrity maps. My next task was to send out a few thousand letters and record the responses. I thought it would be fun to try, and maybe if I was lucky some of the people would respond. But then, almost 20 percent of the people I wrote to, wrote back, and suddenly the dream seemed real. I was being told by hundreds of successful people what they learned in all their lives that was most important.

In essence, I was looking for some insight to help guide me in my own search for what has been the most important thing I've learned so far. I wanted to see what evident patterns or differences in answers there were among different ages, different occupations, and even different sexes—*if there was any at all*. I couldn't find any consistent patterns. Some responses were very individual while others were universally instructive. No one group had a particularly distinctive type of reply.

Most of the quotations I received by mail. There were several occasions, however, when I built up the nerve to approach people in person. I asked people on buses and trains, over the phone, and I even traveled to where people worked. Almost all of the time their first reaction was, "Boy, that's a tough one, can I take a second?" That was not always the case. One time, I attended screenwriter Budd Schulberg's lecture about *On the Waterfront*, at a nearby university. In the question and answer session that followed I nervously asked him my question. The entire audience burst into an uproar. They were laughing and calling out, delighted to see him on the spot, forced to answer such a difficult question. Yet after only a few seconds of hesitation, he was able to answer quite eloquently. Another time, at a Knicks game, I had a friend distract some ushers while I snuck down to courtside at halftime to see Spike Lee, who told me to "Eat your vegetables."

I was not surprised that many people sent me strange and funny quotations. It occurred to me that the people who wrote these witticisms were somehow saying that they learned it was important to have a sense of humor. For example, Terry Gilliam, the director of *The Fisher King*, said he had been told, "Never trust a man in a blue trench coat and never drive when you're dead." Bill Cosby told me "breath." Most people, however, spoke about things that dealt with family, relationships, and values. Many also mentioned the "Golden Rule." In fact, it was the exception to hear from someone who was able to narrow it down to a single thing that was most important. Instead, many gave lists of several that were equally important.

Among the hundreds of form letters, apologies, and preprinted autographs, there were many people who sincerely said that they couldn't answer me. Persistence was definitely required if I was to achieve my goal. For example, I was sent a letter by Katharine Hepburn saying she would like to respond but didn't have the time right then. A few months later, after the second letter, she answered my question. Also, physicist Stephen Hawking was a very tough man to reach. I wrote to him three times in two different countries, and finally, he wrote back. There were also times I felt a personal touch was needed. Actor Adam West responded after I had added an extra long postscript to my standard request. I told him how when I was three years old I really thought I was Batman. To give just one more example, Charles Schulz, the creator of "Peanuts," sent me a letter after I drew a picture of Snoopy asking him to please write back. There were also people who strongly disagreed with what I was doing. They told me in so many words to find out for myself what was important. On the other hand, I got letters from a much larger number of people telling me that my search was an enlightening and worthwhile endeavor.

There was the time I was away at summer camp when I got a phone call from my mom telling me the FBI was looking for me! That's right, the secret service came to my door (dark sunglasses and all), flashed their badges, and asked to speak to me. It seems that one of the people I had written to was John Hinckley, Jr., Ronald Reagan's would-be assassin. Anyway, he had a parole hearing coming up and all his mail was being screened. I guess they thought I was giving him some kind of secret escape code. Eventually they decided I was okay.

One thing that I will surely miss about this project is going to my mailbox every day and opening up letters from famous people from all over the world. I still can't believe they took the time to share these intimate thoughts with a perfect stranger—me! So right now I would like to take the time to say: Thank you.

I would probably say that the most important thing I've learned in life so far is to enjoy life, to make sure you do whatever makes you happy—if it's being successful, having a family, being educated, or helping others, whatever applies to you, just so you like living. Or, I could say that I'm really not sure yet and that's why I wrote this book.

Before you read any further, I would like you to try and think: What is the most important thing you've learned in life?

W hat I have learned from life is to make the most of what you have got."

—*Stephen Hawking, professor of mathematics, physicist, and author*
University of Cambridge
England

K eep your head in the clouds but your feet on the ground. From my tap-dancing Camille Hill to me."

—*Tommy Tune, dancer and choreographer*
New York

Honesty is nothin', compared to decency."

—Jackie Mason, comedian
New York

∞

Don't expect others to do your work for you."

—William Safire, journalist
New York Times
New York

∞

Honesty is the best policy, except when you must tell a very ugly woman she is beautiful."

—Phyllis Diller, comedienne
California

Be curious about life, and cautious with it!"

—*Vincent Price, actor*
California

Ask lots of questions. Don't ever be sure you don't need to ask, to listen, to question your own assumptions."

—*James Michaels, editor*
Forbes *magazine*
New York

What I don't know."

—*Billy Joel, musician*
New York

To relax."

—John Torreano, artist
New York

∾

If you want to do something, try it! The worst anyone you ask for help can do is say no."

—Ann Beatts, author
New York

∾

Keep doing."

—Cy Coleman, Broadway composer
New York

Breath!"

—*Bill Cosby, comedian*
New York

∽

To live every moment in the present. Do it. Risk it. Buy it
if you love it. Loving well takes practice, delicious practice.
If it feels good, it must be good."

—*Gael Greene, food critic*
New York

∽

To appreciate dry cleaning."

—*Irving Greenblatt, hotel owner*
Puerto Rico

Believe you can do anything you want to do if you work hard enough to achieve it. If you believe in yourself so will others."

—Graham Green, First Secretary to the Ambassador of Canada
New York

You make your own luck. Luck is the residue of design."

—Larry King, TV talk show host
Virginia

Empathy."

—Gloria Steinem, author, editor
New York

Luck is an incredibly important element in the mix and unfortunately it's something we can pray and hope for but we really can't depend on its occurrence."

—William Link, TV/movie writer-producer
California

Happiness is not a string of miscellaneous adventures or experiences but an attitude. We either make ourselves miserable, or we make ourselves happy and strong. The amount of work is the same."

—Francesca Reigler, artist
New York

Remember to always dream. More importantly, work hard to make those dreams come true and never give up."

—Dr. Robert D. Ballard, Director
Center for Marine Exploration
Massachusetts

∞

To consider and treat others the way you want to be treated."

—Walter Annenberg, publisher, art collector, and philanthropist
Pennsylvania

∞

To have friends and be nice to them, so we stay friends."

—Tina Trigg, first grader
Sweden

To have a good friend to trust and count on, you must be a friend to them that they can always trust and count on!"

—Ashley Lucero, tenth grader
Texas

Try to take people the way they really mean things, not always the way they sound. It's hard to do!"

—Raquel Welch, actress
California

The importance of one's reputation."

—Tom Wickham, Southold Town Supervisor
New York

That if you try to put yourself in the other guy's shoes—even for a minute—understanding and compassion will come."

—Paul Winfield, actor
California

∾

Do not expect people to behave perfectly—after all, they are people, with all of the faults and frailties of the human condition."

—Donald M. Fehr, Executive Director
Major League Baseball Players Association
New York

To live with other people and make room for their wishes as well as your own. Be compassionate toward weaker people and flexible toward the stronger ones."

—Shallon
U.N. Development
New York

Patience and tolerance and learning it every day."

—Jak Kunstler, auctioneer
Louisiana

The purpose of life is not to win. The purpose of life is to grow and to share. When you come to look back on all that you have done in life, you will get more satisfaction from the pleasure you have brought into other people's lives than you will from the times that you outdid and defeated them."

—Rabbi Harold Kushner
Massachusetts

The biggest disease in life is jealousy."

—Paul Sheldon, taxi driver
New York

Have confidence in your decisions. Make them expeditiously, and stay with them as long as you believe you are correct no matter what others say. However, when you conclude you were in error, do not hesitate to announce the error publicly and change course."

—*Edward I. Koch, former mayor*
New York

You should discover your own truths through thoughtful evaluation of the ideas presented by others."

—*Dewitt McKay, jazz musician*
Pennsylvania

Never be afraid to ask a question, especially of yourself—
discovery is the mission of life."

—Brian Kates, author, journalist
New York

∞

Success is going from failure to failure without losing enthusiasm."

—Danny Glover, actor
California

∞

Pretense is the enemy of happiness."

—Jeff Greenfield, political commentator
New York

It is a quote from Kipling and it states: 'To meet with Triumph and Disaster, and treat those two impostors just the same.' "

—Oleg Cassini, designer
New York

Each person is a V.S.P. (a Very Special Person) because we are each created in the image of God."

—Bishop Desmond Tutu, human rights activist
South Africa

Faith will keep you up."

—*Jake Sherkow, fourth grader*
California

❧

Persevere."

—*Ray Stark, producer*
California

❧

This too shall pass."

—*Barbara Walters, television journalist*
New York

If we don't change, we don't grow. If we don't grow, we are not really living. Growth demands a temporary surrender of security. It may mean a giving up of familiar but limiting patterns, safe but unrewarding work, values no longer believed in, relationships that have lost their meaning. As Dostoevsky put it, 'taking a new step, uttering a new word, is what people fear most.' The real fear should be the opposite course."

—Gail Sheehy, author
New York

Not to give up. If you believe strongly in something and are trying to make a change, the fight to succeed is worth every inch of the way."

—Molly Yard, President
National Organization for Women
Washington, D.C.

It is of primary importance to develop—highly—your sense of proportion: your values, your priorities, and so on. You just have to find out—and the sooner the better—what is important and what isn't, and resist spending your energies and resources on the latter."

—Jack Weaver, musician
California

Know thyself.' And 'to one's own self be true.' Beyond that, I believe we have been given the spark of life which unites us in spirit to all living things. And that must be remembered as we go about our daily business."

—*Dave Brubeck, jazz musician*
Connecticut

Pride, perception, perseverance, persistence, preparation."

—*Wayne Embry, General Manager*
Cleveland Cavaliers
Ohio

Do your best! My guideposts: duty, honor, country."

—*Brent Scowcroft, National Security Adviser*
Washington, D.C.

Commitment alone justifies living. Demand joy. Make
yourself work with joy, even mechanically, and before you
know it, the feeling is real! For it is only in this state that
you can accomplish wonderful things."

—*Nina Foch, actress*
California

Don't be afraid to stick to your convictions."

—Dr. Benjamin Spock, pediatrician and author
Virgin Islands

Never stop until you get what you really want, but first be sure to find out where the men's room is, eventually you will need it."

—Dan Sherkow, film producer
California

W hether you think you can, or you can't, you're right."

—*Ben Cohn and Jerry Greenfield*
Ben & Jerry Ice Cream
Vermont

∽

S et a goal and stick to it. Let nothing interfere with your achieving this objective."

—*Bill Blass, designer*
New York

∽

Y ou can't count on anyone but yourself, otherwise you'll be disappointed."

—*Lori Tartell, registered nurse*
New York

Never trust a man in a blue trench coat. Never drive a car when you're dead. Tom Waits taught me this."

—*Terry Gilliam, film director*
England

❧

Have confidence in your ability and judgment."

—*Dr. Paul Berg, Nobel-Prize winner for Biochemistry*
Stanford University School of Medicine
California

❧

To learn something that no one ever knew before."

—*Dr. Rosalyn S. Yalow, Nobel-Prize winner for Physics*
Virginia

I learned in the Marine Corps: always be on time and to be ready to do what you're supposed to do when you get there."

—*Ed McMahon, entertainer*
California

To be honest and to be clear."

—*Warren Hoge, Assistant Managing Editor*
The New York Times
New York

To honor compassion. The ability to acknowledge and understand or seek to understand other lives is the greatest goal of any man."

—*Jason Alexander, actor*
California

∞

To use my mind and energy to think for myself, and not to ask others to do my work for me."

—*Max Frankel, Executive Editor*
The New York Times
New York

Don't take life for granted."

—*James Perez, army sergeant*
New York

∾

Abandon the urge to simplify everything, to look for formulas and easy answers, and begin to think multidimensionally, to glory in the mystery and paradoxes of life, not to be dismayed by the multitude of causes and consequences that are inherent in each experience—to appreciate the fact that life is complex."

—*M. Scott Peck, psychiatrist and author*
Connecticut

$C_{are.}$"

—*Sidney Sheldon, novelist*
New York

∞

T_{o} open your heart and tell the truth."

—*Don Johnson, actor*
California

∞

T_{urn} the other cheek."

—*Kathleen Sullivan, talk show host*
New York

Life is about sharing."

—*Yoko Ono, artist*
New York

All beings are *one*—with each other and with the earth and
with God."

—*Joan Weaver, musician*
California

Ambition might make you rich, but only people can make
you happy."

—*Andrew Heyward, Producer*
"Eye to Eye"
New York

Set a goal and be perseverant to accomplish it, otherwise you're floating on an ocean without direction."

—*Steve Zeifert, design engineer*
Poland

Never take yourself too seriously."

—*Don Hewitt, Producer*
"60 Minutes"
New York

Life is very, very short and we should savor every minute."

—*Wilma P. Mankiller, Chief of the Cherokees*
Oklahoma

Life is too short to waste a lot of time doing things you really don't want to be doing."

—Bruce Isaacs, hydroponics farmer
New York

&

On location for a film in Mexico, a circle of some of the most famous people in the world gathered one night for dinner: Elizabeth Taylor, Richard Burton, Truman Capote, Ava Gardner, Tennessee Williams, Ray Stark (the producer), and the great director John Huston. They decided to play a game. They would go down the length of the table and, one by one, each person would use one word to describe what they thought was most important in life. As they moved down the line a list of the usual suspects emerged: beauty, wealth, success, fame, knowledge, health, family . . . until it came time for Mr. Huston to speak. He looked around the room at the group, took his cigar out of his mouth, and quietly said, 'Interest. Interest. To be interested in what life has to offer.' "

—*Kevin Spacey, actor*
New York

∾

That love of family, pride in country, and appreciation of the power of God and freedom make for a full life."

—*Marvin Kalb, Director*
John F. Kennedy School of Government
Harvard University
Massachusetts

We should live every day like it is our last, and treat every person with dignity and respect."

—Anne Seymour, Director
Communications and Resource Development
National Victim Center
Texas

Don't eat on a full stomach."

—Ray Dillman, attorney
Florida

Don't ever do anything for money. Money lust has killed more people than the atomic bomb."

—Grey Palast, economist
New York

Nothing in life is unimportant."

—*John Cage, composer*
New York

Never give up, never stop learning, never say anything bad about anybody behind their back, and always remember that good friends are the essence of a good life."

—*John Roland, news anchorman, Fox 5*
New York

Be kind to others, be open-minded to accept everyone for what they are."

—Aparna Guha, college student
Canada

∞

We cannot love others until we love ourselves. We cannot love ourselves until we truly believe that God loves us."

—Kathie Lee Gifford, talk show host, author
New York

The ultimate goal is to improve the quality of life on planet earth."

—*Chalmers F. Sechrist, Assistant Dean*
College of Engineering
University of Illinois at Urbana-Champaign
Illinois

Take nothing for granted!"

—*Fred L. Whipple, astronomer*
Massachusetts

No god, learn meditation, make physical love, don't watch much hi-tech TV, write poetry, read Shakespeare, memorize the Buddhist heart Sutra, make friends, learn the three marks of exceptance and the four noble truths of Buddha Dharma, live as long as you can cheerfully, letting go of your thoughts with each breath."

—Allen Ginsburg, poet
California

To be satisfied with that which you have and to appreciate it."

—Erika Frisch-DeBiasio, ice cream shop owner
Germany

Never go into business with friends."

—*Joshua Gold, disc jockey*
Toronto

∞

I was lucky to be given life—what I get out of it is up to me! (But the support of family and friends can make all the difference!)"

—*Babette Low, therapist*
New York

∞

To help my mom and dad."

—*Kristina Hansen, fifth grader*
New York

My wife, Kate."

—*Julius Guterman, retired builder*
Florida

Spending time with my family; watching my children grow up. Try to make the world a better place; be part of the solution not the problem. Have your work help others. Study—learn—grow."

—*Ted Turner, founder*
CNN and TBS
Georgia
(from an interview by David Frost)

To have a good heart."

—Hamdy Mohamed, taxi driver
Florida

Count your change."

—Joel Farb, comic
England

Show up."

—Victor Neufeld, Producer
"20/20"
New York

Rewards come to those who are willing to work hard for them. First you need the education appropriate to your goal. Then you need the will, dedication, and perseverance to fulfill that dream."

—Dr. Gertrude B. Elion, Scientist Emeritus
Nobel-Prize winner for Pharmacology
Wellcome Research Laboratories, Burroughs Wellcome Co.
North Carolina

I believe that a good education is the key to success. People who read and write well are the ones who are successful."

—Julia Child, cooking expert
Massachusetts

Be the best at what you do and someday you'll get noticed."

—Mike Zaifert, eighth grader
Poland

To be patient, be kind to others, be honest, to be caring."

—Dr. Sharma Ashok, physician
England

To love myself."

—Joan Finkelstein, actress
New York

To understand that a positive and productive life is up to each one of us individually. We are our own realizers. We are our own best teachers. Remember to keep the knowingness that the God source is *within* you. Trust it and your life and love will reflect it."

—*Shirley MacLaine, actress and author*
California

∾

If you think you are beaten, you are;
If you think that you dare not, you don't;
If you'd like to win, but you think you can't,
It's almost certain you won't.
If you think you'll lose, you've lost;

For out in the world you'll find
Success begins with a fellow's will—
It's all in the state of mind.
If you think you are outclassed, you are;
You've got to think high to rise;
You've got to be sure of yourself before
You can ever win a prize.
Life's battles don't always go
To the stronger or faster man;
But soon or late the man who wins
Is the man who thinks he can."

—Unattributed poem submitted by
Arnold Palmer, professional golfer
Pennsylvania

A man can achieve any dream he is capable of conceiving. The only boundaries we have are the ones we place upon our own imaginations!"

—Tom DeFalco, Editor in Chief
Marvel Comics
New York

Follow your dreams and make the most out of every experience."

—David J. Stern, Commissioner
National Basketball Association
New York

If you don't stand for something, you'll fall for anything!"

—James Bond III
Bonded Enterprises Inc.
New York

✿

First, an individual can make a difference in this world. One should not say I am only one person and there is nothing I can do. If you are dedicated, if you are willing to work hard, if your goals contribute to the well-being of our society, you will find others who will join you."

—Fujio Matsuda, Executive Director
Research Corporation of the University of Hawaii
Hawaii

Don't change yourself for anyone."

—*Matt Regan, seventh grader*
New York

Attempting to do things in the right way and working hard at it is the best way to get things done. Applying short-term, quick-fix solutions to problems does not work very well."

—*Tom Osborne, head football coach*
University of Nebraska
Nebraska

This quote by Robert Browning has ruled my life 'Ah, but a man's reach should exceed his grasp or what's a heaven for.' "

—*Susan Israelson, author*
New York

Hard work is important no matter what work it is."

—*Dr. James Buchanon, Nobel-Prize winner for Economics*
Virginia

If we are willing to make the sacrifices necessary to accomplish our goals, nothing can stop us from achieving them."

—Jesse Helms, U.S. Senator from North Carolina
Washington, D.C.

No matter how old a person is, he or she is capable of change—in terms of habits, attitudes, beliefs, feelings, behavior, and so on."

—Dorothy Mulligan, screenwriter
New York

Don't assume that because people are older they're smarter."

—*Bob Wacker, journalist*
New York

To plan ahead. And I'm not talking about two or three weeks, I'm talking about two years and sometimes three years. If you plan ahead and set a goal, with perseverance you will be able to accomplish that goal."

—*David L. Wolper, film producer*
California

One gets out of life what one puts into it."

—*Ed Polcer, musician*
New York

∞

To go to college."

—*Yuelin Xu, medical student*
China

∞

Read Noam Chomsky and Edward Said."

—*Julie Christie, actress*
England

Get an education, get a job, get a receipt."

—Mrs. Dzenkowski, librarian
New York

Don't get carried away by the applause."

—Sebastian Metz, International Coordinator
Citizens Crime Prevention Group, Guardian Angels
New York

Don't fool yourself! Be realistic about your talents and gifts, then apply them with hard work and dedication."

—Harry Wendelstedt, baseball umpire
Florida

Know your limits."

—*Janet Chusmir, Editor*
Miami Herald
Florida

∽

To do something in which you are deeply interested. Work
should be satisfying; something you look forward to doing.
There is a boring aspect to almost everything, but if you
choose to do something worthwhile, that helps people, the
satisfactions outweigh the 'dumb' part."

—*Elaine Benson, art gallery owner*
New York

Be honest and work hard."

—*Paul Volcker, economist*
Princeton University
New Jersey

The paramount importance of family, friendship, and loyalty."

—*Jerry Finkelstein, financier*
New York

Never pay retail."

—*Ira Gasman, lyricist*
New York

To make the most out of life and be happy."

—Chris Mullin, basketball player
Golden State Warriors
California

❧

Live your life as though one day you'll be investigated, because eventually you will be—by yourself. Live your life so that when that time comes you'll like what you see."

—Charles Grodin, actor
Connecticut

You just never know what's around the corner!"

—*Joan Sutherland, opera singer*
New York

When opportunity knocks on your door, accept it."

—*Jane Wyatt, actress*
California

Be Free."

—*Eddie Murphy, actor*
California

Since this is my only life I want to live forever. The only way I can accomplish that is to make a difference in the lives of others."

—*Gina Ginsberg Riggs, Executive Director*
Gifted Child Society, Inc.
New Jersey

When kindness or understanding happens unexpectedly, there is no greater delight."

—*William Bolcom, musician, composer, and educator*
University of Michigan School of Music
Michigan

Mendacity, the fine art of lying to oneself, is perhaps the most terrible of all human failings. If you're able to lie to yourself, you're able to justify hatred, greed, jealousy, avarice, and any other evil. If you learn that you cannot lie to yourself, you have a good shot at being a decent human being."

—*Leon Uris, author*
New York

Through maturity, you can become anyone you want to be."

—*Esteban Vincente, artist*
New York

You have to consider not one but three different things: (1) Yourself—you will feel good about yourself if you spend time doing things you are good at; also, keep in mind that you might, through confusion or temptation, do the wrong thing. Forgive yourself. (2) Those around you—try to do nice things for all those around you. (3) Your place in the universe—be constructive in the community in which you live."

—*Dan Rattiner, Editor*
Dan's Papers
New York

Be kind to others—and be honest."

—*Adam West, actor*
Idaho

To do all things that make one feel comfortable in spirit. To do nothing that harms anyone. In short 'do the right thing.' "

—*Al Sunshine, dentist*
New York

The cheapest gift I have to give is kindness, and it is the best."

—*Bob Kerry, Senator from Nebraska*
Washington, D.C.

∞

Work hard, never lie, and never hurt anybody."

—*Jerry M. Reinsdorf, Chairman*
Chicago White Sox/Chicago Bulls
Illinois

Right is right if nobody does it and wrong is wrong if everybody does it. And I was also told that nothing succeeds like hard work."

—*Ed Bradley, television journalist*
"60 Minutes"
New York

Do what you can and don't hurt other people while you're doing it."

—*Sir Bob Geldof, humanitarian and rock musician*
England

To enhance the lives of those around us."

—Brooke Astor, philanthropist
New York

❧

Lend a helping hand whenever one is needed, and always try forgiving and forgetting whenever you've been done wrong."

—Randy Travis, country music singer
Tennessee

To learn to sacrifice."

—Lindsay Leung, college student
Canada

∾

First you must *know* what you want, then do it with friendly thoughts."

—Christo, artist
New York

∾

To keep your mouth shut."

—Larry Gagosian, art gallery owner
New York

Enjoy the ride—choose the right partner and decide what you really want to do in life and then do it."

—*Eli Wallach, actor*
New York

I am totally responsible for myself and know this is the one and only path to true happiness, success, and freedom."

—*Georgette Mosbacher,*
CEO, President, Georgette Mosbacher Enterprises
New York

Try to be the best you can be. Focus. Concentrate. Trust your instincts and your common sense. . . . Give, and you will receive—open a door for somebody else. The more you share, the more you will have. . . . Don't just make a living, make a life. The possessions you gather do not define you—it's the people you know and love who count."

—*Fred L. Turner, Senior Chairman, McDonalds Corporation*
Illinois

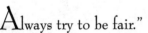

Always try to be fair."

—*James M. Nederlander, theater producer*
New York

To laugh a lot."

—Dr. Donna E. Shalala, Secretary of Health and Human Resources
Washington, D.C.

∽

I never wanted to be anyone else, just Karl. Be yourself and be the best you can be."

—Karl Malone, professional basketball player
Utah Jazz
Utah

∽

To be yourself and tell the truth."

—Lawrence Moroz, attorney
Canada

The ultimate defense against growing old is your dream. Nothing is as real as a dream. Your dream is the path between the person you are and the person you hope to become. Success isn't money. Success isn't power. The criteria for your success are to be found in your dream, in your self. Your dream is something to hold on to. It will always be your link with the person you are today, young and full of hope. If you hold on to it, you may grow old, but you will never be old. And that is the ultimate success."

—*Tom Clancy, author*
New York

Never do anything that builds character."

—*Brian Vaccariello, ninth grader*
New York

I've learned that mankind is basically good. Given opportunity, every individual has the capability of becoming a hero of sorts."

—*Steven Seagal, actor*
California

I wrote ten unsuccessful books before *Eye of the Needle*, and the main thing I learned from those failures was to be a perfectionist. If I do my very best, it might be just good enough."

—Ken Follett, author
England

∾

You have to pay the price. You will find that everything in life exacts a price, and you will have to decide whether the price is worth the prize."

—Sam Nunn, U.S. Senator from Georgia and Chairman,
Senate Committee on Armed Services
Washington, D.C.

My answer is found in this anecdote. The story is told of a father who had twin sons. One son was an optimist, the other a pessimist. On the twins' birthday, while the boys were at school, the father loaded the pessimist's room with every imaginable toy and game. The optimist's room he loaded with horse manure. That night the father passed by the pessimist's room and found him sitting amid his new gifts crying bitterly. 'Why are you crying?' the father asked. 'Because my friends will be jealous, and I'll have to read the instructions, and I'll constantly need batteries, and my toys will get broken,' answered the pessimist. Passing the optimist's room, the father found him dancing for joy in the pile of manure. 'What are you so happy about?' asked the father. To which the optimist replied, 'There's got to be a pony in here somewhere!' "

—*Irving Eskenazi, financial investor*
New York

❦

One learns from life, as one learns in school: from one's own efforts. There's a classical view that a child is not like a vessel into which one pours knowledge and understanding, but like a plant that one can, perhaps, help to flourish in its own way."

—*Noam Chomsky, theoretical linguist*
Massachusetts Institute of Technology
Massachusetts

Extraordinary high expectation levels are required if you are to compete with the best and be successful. Never be satisfied to accept things as they are."

—David T. Kearns, Deputy Secretary
U.S. Department of Education
Washington, D.C.

∞

The measure of one's success is not the wealth accumulated, the shrines erected, the records broken, or the battles won. It is the inner strength which builds each day through hard work, integrity, and a respect for mankind."

—Melvin Simon, owner
Indiana Pacers
Indiana

Explaining things to others is inseparable from explaining something to one's self. Some people call the first teaching, the second research. But they are one."

—Dr. Roald Hoffmann, Nobel-Prize winner for Chemistry
Cornell University
New York

Don't be afraid to ask the stupid question."

—Ronnie Wacker, journalist
New York

To be happy and successful in life means that the amount of information that you will need to remember in a lifetime does not nearly approach the amount that you will need to forget."

—Randy Reinhart, musician and teacher
New Jersey

Work hard. Work harder than the person sitting next to you."

—Ben Bradlee, Managing Editor
The Washington Post
Washington, D.C.

Satisfaction is most likely to be achieved when projects involve hard work and thought rather than merely good fortune or the efforts of others."

—Sam Zagoria, professor
Florida Atlantic University
Florida

❧

Standards of Excellence: (1) Pride, (2) Desire, (3) Teamwork, (4) Attention to detail, (5) Follow-through."

—John C. Marous, Chairman and CEO
Westinghouse Electric Corporation
Pennsylvania

The only time you have to succeed is the last time you try."

—*Philip H. Knight, Chairman and CEO*
NIKE, Inc.
Oregon

∽

The creative potential is innate in every person and we should struggle to make it function in our lives."

—*Krishna Reddy, artist and educator*
New York

W hen you fail in an endeavor, don't blame others; it's more likely that you were partly at fault."

—Martin Harwit, Director
National Air and Space Museum
Smithsonian Institution
Washington, D.C.

∞

 T o never stop learning. About anything and everything, anybody and everybody, our earth and our universe, our thoughts and our feeling, and hopefully the ability to express in motion or verbalize joyfully, 'the wonder of it all.' "

—Jeanette Gilbert, real estate investor
Arizona

There is so much more to learn. Each of us has the opportunity to sample the accumulated wisdom and beauty of the human experience, an infinite, never-ending feast for the mind and heart. Once we come to understand that there are no boundaries or limitations, we can look forward to a lifetime of spiritual and intellectual enrichment."

—*Dr. Sidney M. Clearfield, Executive Vice President*
B'nai B'rith International
Washington, D.C.

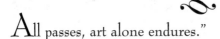

All passes, art alone endures."

—*Lili Lakich, artist and founder*
Museum of Neon Art
California

There's a long life of work ahead. When you finish school, give yourself a year of adventure—and keep notes."

—*Jack Rosenthal, Editor*
The New York Times
New York

That the death of someone who's special or someone you care dearly about is a tough thing that sometimes in your life you have to deal with."

—*Amy Waskiewicz, sixth grader*
New York

That the world is not as wonderful as we are first told and taught, but, on the other hand, it may not be as horrible as we think, and, most importantly, we should never stop striving to make it better. I also learned that my mother was right about brushing my teeth after every meal and to lay off the sticky candies."

—*David Brenner, comedian*
New York

Being an activist. Every effort helps, even if it is a finger in the dike to hold back the flood."

—*Budd Shulberg, author, screenwriter*
New York

That pain hurts in many ways."

—Mike Wheeler, sixth grader
New York

⌘

That we must cling to life with every fiber of our being while yet we may—allowing none of its precious moments to pass by unawares. But, paradoxically, to muster the inner strength to surrender life's gifts when we must. Life confronts us with many losses and we have to learn to cope with them as well."

—Rabbi Alexander M. Schindler, President
Union of American Hebrew Congregations
New York

Run from that myth that material success will bring you happiness. And ignore its counterpart, the lie that the world loves you. The crowd loves a football coach when he succeeds on the fourth-and-one call they were screaming for. But where are they when it fails, when the team loses, when you've made a mistake that puts a ball game out of reach? That's when you learn what the world really thinks of you. Cast your lot with the God in whom there is no change, neither shadow of turning. He loves you as much when you're on the bottom as when you're on top, and it's even clearer and more real to you when you're suffering."

—Joe Gibbs, coach
Washington Redskins
Washington, D.C.

All I can tell you is: get used to it, son!"

—*Milos Forman, film director*
New York

❧

To accept graciously, the inevitable."

—*Ricardo Montalban, actor*
California

❧

Learn to take one day at a time and not to worry about to-morrow."

—*Ann W. Richards, Governor*
Texas

Death is not easy to deal with and life is hard."

—Courtney Martin, sixth grader
New York

Things change."

—Joe Townsend, owner
Insurance company
New York

I believe in continuity and change."

—I. M. Pei, architect
New York

Keep cool."

—*Larry Rivers, artist*
New York

∞

Don't push."

—*Brian Wagner, kindergartner*
New York

∞

Don't take money from strangers."

—*Mr. Henry, officer*
Diplomat Security, U.N.
New York

To learn lessons from the ordinary experiences of everyday life—from everything we do and say and think and feel, and, as important, from everything that those around us do and say and think and feel. We need to learn—from the good times and the bad, from both success and failure, when people help us and when they disappoint us, when we're proud of ourselves and not so proud, when we're generous or mean, courageous or cowardly."

—*Mario Cuomo, Governor*
New York

Life is not a path of coincidence, happenstance, or luck, but rather an unexplainable, meticulously charted course for one to touch the lives of others and make a difference in the world."

—*Barbara Dillingham, English teacher*
New York

A love of nature and an enjoyment of the world around me."

—*Lady Bird Johnson, former First Lady*
Texas

It is always important to do what you think is right in all circumstances. Being kind never hurt anyone. And in today's world, it's more important than ever to preserve the environment for ourselves and future generations and to stop the polluters!"

—Peter Bahouth, Executive Director
Greenpeace
Washington, D.C.

By living close to nature, abiding by its laws and being amazed at its different manifestations, one cannot help but be happy."

—Pierre Matte, librarian
Canada

It's important to remember, although it's against our nature to, that we humans are not the center of life. We must make a balance on earth and take our place among the animals, who are equally important. We must respect their space, and all of nature."

—John Williams, conductor
Boston Symphony Orchestra
Massachusetts

The purpose of life, all life, is to have offspring and keep them secure and healthy long enough to have secure and healthy offspring of their own."

—Tom Wolfe, author
New York

Set short-term as well as long-term goals. Organize your studies and your hopes for a job/career with that in mind. Be realistic about your expectations. Don't waste time worrying about what you haven't or can't accomplish."

—*Cele G. Lalli, Editor in Chief*
Modern Bride *magazine*
New York

In order to survive you must learn to adapt, maneuver, and above all else stay committed."

—*Willie Nelson, singer*
Utah

Nothing is more important than making a contribution toward a better world for future generations. When you have a child you are affirming your belief that humankind will endure and will overcome the many serious problems that confront it."

—*Peter Zheutlin, spokesperson*
International Physicians for the Prevention of Nuclear War

The treatment must not be worse than the disease."

—*Dr. Alvin S. Tierstein, pulmonary specialist*
Mount Sinai Medical Center
New York

Happiness runs in a circular motion. Relax, be cool, enjoy nature."

—*Hulk Hogan, professional wrestler*
Connecticut

Listen."

—*Bill Price, Jr., Town Justice*
New York

To appreciate even tiny happenings like a beautiful flower or a nice day."

—*Anne Vilemsons, eleventh grader*
Sweden

We are put here for a blink of an eyelash. We don't have very much time to make a difference, so we'd better start now."

—*Judy Polcer, actress*
New York

To delegate my time as far as priorities go."

—*Joan Rivers, comedienne*
New York

Isaiah Berlin, in his classic essay on Dostoevsky and Tolstoy, chose to contrast two human categories as the hedgehogs and the foxes. Berlin cites the Greek proverb, 'The fox knows many things, but the hedgehog knows one great thing.' The hedgehog relates everything to a single central vision. In this category Berlin places Dante, Plato, and Dostoevsky. The foxes pursue many ends, often unrelated and even contradictory. Berlin's foxes are Shakespeare, Aristotle, Montaigne, Pushkin, and Tolstoy. The hedgehog seeks certitude, the fox seeks a better understanding. Whether you turn out to be a hedgehog or a fox, take it from a fox that you would be well advised to follow your instincts and your opportunities and to grab the golden ring as it passes you."

—*William H. Luers, President*
Metropolitan Museum of Art
New York

Life is too serious to take seriously."

—*Carol Burnett, comedienne, actress,*
California

Designate priorities; accept challenges; prepare in advance; delegate as much as possible; return phone calls; answer letters and inquiries; show up, dressed and ready to participate; be scrupulously polite; and be definite and firm in the most diplomatic way about one's goals."

—*Barbara Tober, Editor in Chief*
Bride's Magazine
New York

To keep trying. And then keep trying again."

—*Dianne Feinstein, U.S. Senator from California*
Washington, D.C.

The best revenge is to live a good life."

—*Kervin Simms, entertainment attorney*
Florida

∽

True inner happiness is not a thing we can possess at all times. We must constantly strive for it. A person cannot be truly happy if those around him are not happy. He cannot be happy if he has not done a good job, if he has been selfish or untrue in love, if he has been unkind."

—*Ellen Wasson Thomson, real estate broker*
New York

Always be optimistic."

—Bowen Blair, President
Art Institute of Chicago
Illinois

Never refuse cash."

—Scott DePetris, eleventh grader
New York

Love is the question and the answer."

—Tyne Daly, actress
New York

W ith all the achievement that we strive for—the ambition
and desire—without love there is no meaning to
living."

—*John Lone, actor*
New York

T he message Jesus left his disciples: 'Love ye one another,
even as I have loved you.' "

—*Julie Harris, actress*
Massachusetts

D on't hit other people."

—*Kyle Van Duzer, kindergartner*
New York

Those who produce should share in the profits."

—*Ewing M. Kauffman, owner*
Kansas City Royals
Missouri

∞

To have friends."

—*Elaine Steinbeck, widow of John Steinbeck*
New York

Being kind, considerate of others, and honest is the greatest 'golden thread' to hold the home, community, nation, and world together."

—Joe Liles, Executive Director
Society for Preservation and Encouragement of Barber Shop Quartet Singing
Wisconsin

Stop and carefully review what you see or hear instead of jumping to conclusions. Many situations are not what they initially appear to be."

—Carol Brown, nurse
New York

Listening to other people and not rushing to answers about things. Life is very complex and complicated, and no one person can be sure he or she is right. Sharing is essential."

—*Jason McManus, Editor in Chief of Magazine Group*
Time Inc.
New York

People aren't always what they turn out to be. They act like they're really hot. They either act like something big or they act like something small. Either way they always act like someone they're not."

—*Briana Windmuller, sixth grader*
New York

Everything is, at its basis, mental."

—Randolf Crossfield, math teacher
School of Performing Arts
New York

∞

I'll give you a quote from Nietzsche: 'If a man have a strong faith he can indulge in the luxury of skepticism.' "

—Kurt Vonnegut, author
New York

That certainty is the enemy of true knowledge. Knowledge is a process, a journey toward, not an arrival. People who believe they possess certainty are capable of any atrocity, ranging from the concentration camps of the Nazis to the cross burnings of the KKK. Because they are certain they are right, these people feel they can justify any act of subhuman cruelty. Throughout history, it has been the doubters, the assailers of accepted truth, who have moved the species forward. A corollary to this thought is that the only thing you can truly learn in life is the depth of your own ignorance."

—*Al Goldstein, Publisher*
Screw *magazine*
New York

With God's grace everything is possible."

—Thomas A. Murphy, Director
General Motors
Michigan

∾

Everyone was created equal."

—Chris Blackburn, sixth grader
New York

∾

Nobody is perfect."

—Paul Grattan, fifth grader
New York

To be careful crossing the street."

—*Graham Holly Taggert, kindergartner*
New York

Not to react but to think."

—*Dennis Mulligan, retired police detective*
New York

To follow your intuition, listen to your heart, and act on it. But, when in doubt, do nothing!"

—*Jane Alexander, actress, Chairwoman, National Endowment for the Arts*
New York

Keep going—whatever—always."

—Katharine Hepburn, actress
New York

❧

Savoir vivre, which means knowing how to live. The world of our life offers many wonderful joys, from the beaches to the hugs of your family, from the excitement of travel to the pleasures of reading, talking, and being funny. Life should be adventurous, not planned and safe, and the smarter you are the better an adventurer you can be."

—Martin Gottfried, drama critic and author
New York

Row, row, row your boat gently down the stream, merrily, merrily, merrily, merrily, life is but a dream.' They teach this to us very young because it takes so long to learn."

—Bruce Joel Rubin, screenwriter, director
California

∾

I think that every person should be able to enjoy life. Try to decide what you most enjoy doing, and then look around to see if there is a job for which you could prepare yourself that would enable you to continue having this sort of joy."

—Linus Pauling, scientist
Linus Pauling Institute of Science and Medicine
California

What's important to me is what John Lennon told me: Life is what happens while you're busy making other plans. I agree, but equally important is that an active life, with a diversity of experiences, opens you up to various avenues. In other words: Don't be one note, be a symphony."

—*Joe Franklin, talk show host*
New York

To read—because it will take you beyond yourself. To love, to give, to create—for the same reason."

—*Bonnie Bauman, artist*
New York

D rawing letters."

—Elienn, kindergartner
New York

T hose who developed interests seemed to enjoy a high-energy hum that carried them through the years with a snap and a smile."

—Barry Farber, radio talk show host
New York

T o devote yourself to your school studies and read the great thinkers of the past."

—Judith Crist, film critic
New York

Never to pass judgment on another human being without having the ability to see life through that person's eyes."

—*Marla Maples Trump, model*
New York

∞

To respect and show that respect to and for *all* people. To maintain a positive outlook on life. To maintain a sense of humor. Take what you do seriously, but don't take yourself seriously."

—*James Wood, Chairman*
American Bible Society
New York

Rita Mae Brown, a well-known author, said, 'If I had to give anyone advice, it would be to live at least one year of your life completely alone. Whoever you are. If you can't do it, you're in trouble.' This position is a more dramatic one than I would take, but it touches on something I feel is of primary importance. You must have a sense of self-completeness, of autonomy, of independence, or, if you will, of confident solitude. It is only after you establish for yourself that you don't 'need' anyone else in an emotional way that you can then build strong, healthy, and durable relationships with all the other people in your life."

—*Anthony D. Nolde, jazz musician*
Pennsylvania

A human being is a partner in G-d's creation and that just as man needs G-d, so does G-d need man and that part of man's assignment is to be an active partner and to help complete G-d's work."

—*Rabbi Marvin Hier, Dean*
Simon Wiesenthal Center
California

T o trust in God's love and believe that He will take care of me. To not let myself become anxious about the past or the future, and to deal with the people and situations that are in the now."

—*Father Michael Manning, religious leader*
California

How much injustice exists in life and that it is the duty of each of us to fight against injustice and to help others."

—*Gloria Allred, attorney-at-law*
California

∾

To fight for freedom."

—*Ali Shahir, printer*
Iran

∾

Just before George Bernard Shaw died someone approached him in this manner: 'Mr. Shaw you have known all the great men of your time, the artists, the writers, the statesmen; you have an entrée into royalty, you have wined and dined with those who have shaped the destiny of the world in your generation. Now, Mr. Shaw, if you could be born again and relive your life as anyone of your choice, who would it be?' Without a moment's hesitation, Mr. Shaw said, 'If I could relive my life in the role of anyone I choose to be, I would want to be the man that George Bernard Shaw could have been but wasn't.' Here was a man who by all ordinary standards of performance was the greatest. And yet he was dissatisfied. He realized how much more he could have been."

—*Dwight F. Damon, D.C., President*
National Guild of Hypnotists
New Hampshire

To honor my parents, develop self-discipline and perseverance, nurture intellectual curiosity, display courtesy and respect toward others, maintain the highest possible level of
personal integrity, be compassionate, and enjoy the self-grat-
ification of public service."

—Dr. Michael E. DeBakey, heart surgeon and Chancellor
Baylor College of Medicine
Texas

∞

The importance of humility. We need the humility to
know that truth can be ephemeral, that this can be but one
version of the truth."

—Ken Auletta, journalist and author
New York

That living is a continuous learning process. The world is a fascinating place and the more you find out the more you want to find out!"

—*Patricia Wennerstrom, teacher*
Sweden

Get an education. That will be your tool chest. With that you will be able to build."

—*Phillip V. Sanchez*
former Ambassador to Honduras and Colombia
Publisher, Noticias del Mundo
New York

If you genuinely seek to know the secret of life study cosmology and its extension, biology."

—*Thomas A. Sebeok, professor*
Research Center for Language & Semiotic Studies
Indiana University
Indiana

Counting numbers."

—*Bonnie Aldcroft, kindergartner*
New York

The outside world doesn't have a lot to offer. You have to make your own heaven in your own home."

—Bette Midler, singer and actress
California
(from an article in Vanity Fair*)*

No man is an island."

—Howard C. Talbot, Jr., Director
National Baseball Hall of Fame and Museum
New York

Cultivate friendship, it is not often found and takes time to prove itself. Once found, sustain it as if your life depended upon it. It does."

—*Ted Kavanau, television journalist*
New York

I have always tried to treat the *little guy* the same as the *big guy*. But the 'team guy' was always *my guy*!"

—*Jerry Burns, Coach*
Minnesota Vikings
Minnesota

*E*xpress *yourself* in life and in all things you do. Don't live to *impress*!"

—*Imogene Coca, comedienne*
New York

*K*eep a sense of humor. Try to be as intelligent as possible—but don't take yourself too seriously."

—*Wendy Wasserstein, playwright*
New York

*R*ead."

—*P. H. Labalme, educator and administrator*
New Jersey

A person's relationship with the Lord; no matter what, you should guard that relationship because it is so very special."

—Sandi Patti, gospel singer
Indiana

Happiness is not a warm puppy or a fire on a cold night. It is not the beach at dawn or the other things that people say would make them happy. The deep, deep happiness that transcends all else comes from knowing God and, in turn, from being known by Him."

—Reverend Pat Robertson, evangelist
Virginia

Perfection is never possible but striving for perfection gives one the satisfaction of doing one's best no matter what the outcome."

—*R. W. Brown, science teacher*
New York

To hate incompetence."

—*Ben Foti, chief videotape editor*
Fox 5
New York

The value of teamwork. Seeking out, listening to, and valuing the opinions of others—and then making up your mind—is essential."

—William A. Schreyer, Chairman and CEO
Merrill Lynch
New York

That nothing comes from doing nothing, and that one has to work hard to achieve what one wants to be."

—Bess and Isaac Fleishman, retired real estate investors
Florida

Do right. Do the best you can. Treat others the way you would want to be treated."

—Lou Holtz, head football coach
University of Notre Dame
Indiana

Life is immeasurably enriched by living by the Golden Rule—namely, 'Do unto others as you would have them do unto you.' "

—Dr. Franklin Murphy, Chairman
National Gallery of Art
Smithsonian Institution
Washington, D.C.

Keep your temper, be patient with those whose knowledge may not equal your own. Try to be a model of decency because in so doing you are not only helping yourself, but you are an example to others. Don't forget that there is a time to speak and a time to listen and each is all important."

—*Theodore J. LaBrecque, retired judge*
New Jersey

You must have patience, be unemotional, and pick a good lawyer."

—*Barbara Ann Camp, medical assistant*
California

Striving to achieve the ultimate equality of mankind."

—*Donald Seawell, lawyer, publisher, and Arts Center executive*
Colorado

If it's called 'the house salad,' it's no good."

—*David Mamet, playwright and film director*
Massachusetts

Author Leo Rosten once said, 'I think the purpose of life is to be useful, to be responsible, to be compassionate. It is, above all . . . to stand for something, to have made some difference that you lived at all.' "

—Pat Henry, President
National PTA
Illinois

To maintain your respect for other people and maintain your respect for yourself. Accept your faults—all humans have them, but work to improve them, adjust to them and work around them."

—Dr. Augustus A. White III, spinal surgeon
Harvard Medical School
Massachusetts

Not to acknowledge *any* 'sacred cows' in my own personal life, nor in my community. No unthinking loyalty to anything or anyone, flag, country, community, religion, head of state, art form, or behavior pattern, should block off honest discussion and if need be outright rejection."

—Donald Redford, Director
Department of Near Eastern Studies
University of Toronto
Canada

Do not talk to strangers."

—Kevin Grattan, sixth grader
New York

Y ou can't really trust anybody. If you tell something to somebody and you tell them not to tell, it really ends up leaking out."

—*Krista Finne, sixth grader*
New York

T o be careful."

—*Abigail Sherkow, preschooler*
California

W ear a condom."

—*Dan Holmes, eleventh grader*
New York

Not all people are the same. What I mean is that there are bad people and good people and I have to watch out because of the bad people."

—*Jill Schondebare, sixth grader*
New York

Never give in, no matter how bleak or dark things are."

—*Sam Bisconti, Director of Personnel*
School for Deaf and Blind
Florida

Never give up."

—*Judy Collins, singer*
New York

∾

Never say no."

—*Janet Lehr, art gallery owner*
New York

∾

Take risks."

—*H. Michael Zal, psychiatrist and author*
Pennsylvania

There's more to life than a tiny tush and you don't die
from embarrassment."

—*Carole Shaw, Editor*
Big Beautiful Woman Magazine
California

∞

If you want love, you have to give love."

—*Dame Barbara Cartland, author*
England

∞

Forgiveness! P.S.: It's the secret of life."

—*Michael Moriarty, actor*
New York

Getting along with people from many backgrounds and interests is most important if you are going to be involved in society in any way. We are interdependent upon one another."

—Jack Pluckhan, Vice President
Panasonic Corporation
New Jersey

How to play outside."

—Ginelle Born, kindergartner
New York

To love and respect people, all kinds of people, the good and the bad, for they are all God's creation."

—Norman Vincent Peale, minister
Peale Center for Christian Living
New York

Relationships with other people. Cherishing these relationships has made my life incredibly rich."

—Barbara Bush, former First Lady
Washington, D.C.

To give first priority in my time and energy to my loved ones—my family and close friends. They are life's meaning and cushion. Career is second. In career, the most important lesson is to work hard and be persistent."

—Leslie Gelb, Editor
The New York Times
New York

That who we are and how we think of ourselves is defined by human relationships."

—Donald E. Peterson, retired chairman
Ford Corporation
Michigan

Avoid human beings."

—*Tama Janowitz, author*
New York

To be good to and to take care of other people and animals."
—*Tali Trigg, third grader*
Sweden

Don't drink, don't smoke, don't take drugs. Seize the moment. Wealth is a state of mind. Life is there for the taking."

—*Mark Kostabi, artist*
New York

If I only knew then what I know now and conversely, in contradiction, the older I am the less I know. The more I know the less I know. How is that for confusing a thirteen-year-old kid."

—Robert DeNiro, actor, director, and producer
New York

My experience is that nothing you learn is ever wasted; it is what you do not know that can hurt you. The willingness to be curious about everything you encounter is a habit of mind that will serve you well."

—Dr. H. Keith H. Brodie, President
Duke University
North Carolina

Eat your vegetables."

—*Spike Lee, actor and director*
New York

∾

I really believe that by employing the KISS formula I can break down any large problem that I may come across and with commonsense reasoning solve that problem.
KISS=Keep It Simple, Stupid. Oops, I forgot, only root for the Celtics and the Red Sox."

—*Wayne DePetris, owner*
Insurance company
New York

Fill every moment with anything that is not a waste of time: pleasure, learning, reevaluating, the arts, science, philosophy, and so on. The worst thing that can happen to a person when he comes to the end of his life is to suddenly know that he has not participated in it fully, that he has wasted his time, has not devoured all the wonders consciousness affords us."

—Edward Albee, playwright
New York

There will be no success or *real* reward without risk. Do it!"

—*Ellen Levine, Editor in Chief*
Redbook *magazine*
New York

☙

Cry not for ignorance as a salty river contains no fresh answer to its solution."

—*Dr. Stephen Kaplan, vampire researcher*
New York

☙

Go ask that guy over there."

—*Benny Waakkay*
New Zealand Mission to the U.N.
New York

There is a God."

—*Mordechai Levy, founder*
Jewish Defense Organization
New York

Imperious Caesar, dead and turn'd to clay, Might stop a hole to keep the wind away. O that that earth which kept the world in awe, Should patch a wall t'expel the [winter's] flaw!" (*Hamlet*, Act V, Scene 1)

—*Harvey Greenstein, photographer*
New Jersey

I believe that there is a reason for everything even though I do not understand it."

—Frances Mulhall, fifth-grade teacher
New York

❧

Fight chaos with beauty and order."

—Helen Kayn, real estate broker
New Mexico

❧

To learn as much as you can about the world around you, including yourself."

—Herbert A. Hauptman, Ph.D., President
Medical Foundation of Buffalo, Inc.
New York

As to the lessons of life, I can't improve on some lines from a Western movie called *Missouri Breaks*. Two cutthroats with murderous designs on each other are sharing a campfire. One is strumming a guitar and singing an old gospel song called 'Life Is Like Mountain Railroad.' He stops and asks the other fellow in a taunting manner, 'Is life really like a mountain railroad?' 'Naw,' the other replies. 'Then what is life like?' asks the first character. 'Mister,' came the reply, 'life ain't like nothing I ever heard of before.' Also, I owe to Sidney Hook a thought. From him I learned the difference between a truth and a deep truth. A deep truth is a truth the converse of which is equally true.

For example, it is true, as Santayana said, that 'Those who cannot remember the past are condemned to repeat it.' Yet it is equally true that those who do remember the past may not know when it is over. That is deep truth."

—*Lane Kirkland, President*
AFL-CIO
Washington, D.C.

You'll never really know what happiness is unless you have something to compare it to. Remember to accept the lows and gain knowledge from them without giving up."

—*Lee Iacocca, former Chairman and CEO*
Chrysler Corporation
Michigan

To know that our 'book of life' will eventually have many 'chapters' in it and I think that that is kind of neat because each 'chapter' has its own discoveries and opportunities. I've learned to approach each 'chapter' with an openness to discovery and belief in myself and my loved ones and then let it happen."

—*William F. Kieschnick, former President and CEO*
ARCO
California

Be a servant, be compassionate, be caring and loving. Be a real person."

—*John David Mohn, musician*
New Jersey

There should be at least three cardinal rules for success in personal achievement, whatever the field may be: (1) Complete passionate devotion to whatever field you have chosen. (2) The need to concentrate, to the exclusion of all else, when working on, thinking about, or executing whatever discipline you have chosen. (3) An utter pitiless sense of self-criticism, far greater than that which any outsider could give."

—Isaac Stern, violinist and President
Carnegie Hall
New York

It is a good idea to be ambitious, to have goals, to want to be good at what you want to do, but it is a terrible mistake to let drive and ambition get in the way of being a nice person who cares about other people and takes the trouble to treat them with kindness and decency. The point is not that they will then be nice to you. The point is that you will feel better about yourself."

—Dr. Robert M. Solow, Nobel-Prize winner for Economics
Massachusetts Institute of Technology
Massachusetts

To tolerate ambiguity. People don't feel very comfortable with uncertainty in their lives, and they often respond by taking an action—any action—to resolve it. That's usually a mistake; many problems tend to resolve themselves, and living with a difficult challenge often makes one better able to respond to it successfully."

—Donald Kennedy, President
Stanford University
California

Having learned nothing in life I cannot tell a thirteen-year-old anything he does not already know. If, however, you were a fish I would advise you to stay in the water."

—*Robert Altman, film director*
New York

Money and all that is connected to it are impediments and stumbling blocks along the path to truth. 'So will you follow daydreams or will you follow wealth; and how can you find your fortune if you cannot find yourself?' [Gordon Lightfoot, 'Sit Down Young Stranger,' c. 1972]"

—*William L. Moore*
The Fair-Witness Project, Inc.
California

The journey is not yet over."

—*Professor Wangari Maathal, coordinator*
Green Belt Movement
Kenya

My experience in recent years, because of my cancer, is vastly different from that of the prior years of my life. My new experience now focuses on people I love and those who love me."

—*Randy Guterman, construction designer*
New York

I believe life is the best gift God gave to us. We are all born with the equipment necessary to lead a full, happy, and successful life. So it is the reason I keep up my good spirit hoping there will be better days to come."

—Carmen Monroy, baby-sitter
New York

∽

To be yourself."

—Patricia Schroeder, U.S. Congresswoman from Colorado
Washington, D.C.

Like Cyrano, I ask simply 'To sing, to laugh, to dream, to walk in my own way and be alone. Free, with an eye to see things as they are, . . . At a word, a Yes, a No, To fight—or write. To travel any road, under the sun, under the stars, . . . Never to make a line I have not heard, In my own heart; yet, with all modesty, To say: My soul, be satisfied with flowers, With fruit, with weeds even; but gather them, in the one garden you may call your own.' "

—*David Puttnam, filmmaker*
England

Life is a search for truth, and there is no truth (Chinese proverb). All that matters is to love your family, and to love your work."

—*Gregory Peck, actor*
California

Good things often happen to good people with patience."

—*Jeffrey Lyons, film critic*
New York

Life is only rarely as painful as your worst fears, and over time you can recover from even deep despair, but it's a never-ending job. And despite all objective criteria to the contrary, there is a spiritual realm that encompasses all being. While undefinable, it exists and can be experienced within our limited perception."

—Steve Bauman, publisher
New York

In art there are no rules."

—Gene Saks, director
New York

A good education is essential to personal and professional growth. My parents also instilled in me the importance of honesty, respecting others, and the need to 'think before you leap.' "

—*John D. Rockefeller IV, U.S. Senator from West Virginia*
Washington, D.C.

❧

Y ou alone are responsible for achieving a satisfying life. Don't think it's only a dress rehearsal—this is it!"

—*Jerome Puchkoff, Chairman and CEO*
American Allied Industries
New York

Anything in life is possible if you make it happen. We are all better than we think. Daily exercise is probably the most important habit to acquire."

—Jack LaLanne, exercise instructor
California

No one gets out of this world alive, so the time to live, learn, care, share, celebrate, and love is *now*."

—Dr. Leo Buscaglia, author
New York

Just try to get through life with generosity to others."

—*Jacques D'Ambois, dance instructor*
New York

How to make friends."

—*Brian Warper, kindergartner*
New York

To be true to oneself."

—*Richard Zanuck, film producer*
California

We are not here by cosmic accident. Conscience is a supernatural gift and a compass for conducting our lives. We ignore it at our own peril. Take responsibility, duty, and loyalty very seriously. Develop and keep your sense of humor about life."

—*Fred Zinnemann, film director and producer*
England

To revere and respect creativity. The products of creativity set human beings apart."

—*Caril Dreyfuss McHugh, art consultant and writer*
New York

It is not the possessions, awards, your name up in bright lights—that all fades quickly. Instead, it is the people whose lives you have touched and hopefully made better, as well as the lasting memory of things we've done to help make the world a better place."

—*Marty Richards, broadway producer*
New York

Give generously, without thought of the return."

—*Libby Trigg, mother and grandmother*
Florida

Appreciating when you have it good is an art."

—Judy Ahrens, photojournalist
New York

Never dwell on bitterness, envy, or despair, but rather share your good fortune."

—Neboya Brashich, Foreign Service Officer
Africa

There are no short cuts to achieving anything worthwhile."

—John Williams, President
National Scrabble Association
New York

Talk is cheap, but you can't buy it back."

—*Nancy Lee Baxter, songwriter*
New York

Whoever started it all had some nerve."

—*Jeanette Hendler, fine arts dealer*
New York

Learn to suspect easy answers."

—*Edwin Honig, educator and poet*
Brown University
Rhode Island

First: Pay your rent on time. The second thing is make sure of your premise for everything you do. Ask yourself always, 'Why am I doing this?' "

—Jimmy Breslin, author and columnist
New York

It is not wrong to spell out unfairness in others as long as they deserve it, but save your unkind words and opinions for the moments when they are applicable and not unreasonably brutal. Offer your sympathy when it is due and do not tell a lie. Give love where it is due."

—Craig Claiborne, food critic and author
New York

If more people practiced the Golden Rule we would not face the tragic conditions of war and famine that so many in the world today experience."

—John R. Albers, Chairman and CEO
Dr. Pepper–7 Up
Texas

My Bible tells me 'What does it profit a man to gain the whole world then to lose his soul.' I don't want to get wrapped up in the worldly things or what I can get in this old earth, but I want to concentrate on things that are eternal."

—Steven A. Smith, custodian
New York

My feelings are best expressed by quoting the English poet Hilaire Belloc: 'From quiet homes and first beginning, out to the undiscovered ends, there's nothing worth the wear of winning, but laughter and the love of friends.' "

—William Rossa Cole, poet and anthropologist
New York

It is our nature to be governed by the forces of logic and il-logic. Be somewhat malleable to the fates and circumstances that you encounter. You may not always get the desired results, but you should benefit by entertaining the natural rhythm of human intercourse."

—Paul Stewart, management executive
New York

Oddly, it came to me while reading about Stoicism: Zeno, Epictetus, the emperor Marcus Aurelius. From these men's writings I learned, rather suddenly, that you don't have to hate anyone. No matter how deplorable someone's actions, no matter how you might spend much of your energy opposing, blocking, frustrating his works—which you may rightly perceive to be evil—you don't have to hate the individual. We only hate what we fear, and this realization freed me from fear and hatred."

—Hugh Downs, host and commentator
"20/20"
Arizona

Character, self-discipline, and a willingness to work hard pay off in many ways."

—*Liz Claiborne, fashion designer*
New York

Every day I learn something new."

—*Holly Solomon, art gallery owner*
New York

The answer is not in this book, but in the reader."

—*Tom Stoppard, playwright*
London

To give the highest value to a particular, unique experience, and to avoid abstractions."

—*Wolf Kahn, artist*
New York

∽

Follow your passion and be true to your instincts. Never follow the crowd, always be yourself."

—*Michael Fuchs, Chairman*
HBO
New York

∽

Years ago I made a speech to the North Carolina Writers' Conference, going on and on portentously about literature. When I had finished, Jonathan Daniels, then the editor of the *Raleigh News and Observer* and one of our state's foremost writers, came up to me, shook a finger in my face, and said, 'Young man, never be a solemn ass.' "

—*Tom Wicker, author and columnist*
Vermont

∾

To listen to what other people say before I answer them. This may sound silly, but most people start to formulate their reply before the other person is finished. This often results in missing the true point of what the other person has to say."

—*Michael Field, Chairman*
The Art Institute of Chicago
Illinois

To learn a great deal about our country and the values of our democratic system of government."

—*Lowell Weicker, Jr., Governor*
Connecticut

A person's family, the one we come from and the one we later create are the most important elements of life."

—*Michael Rushford, President*
Criminal Justice Legal Foundation
California

1) There's no substitute for the Golden Rule. The corollary to the Golden Rule is don't cut corners, even if you don't think anybody will notice. You'll notice! (2) Get absolutely as much education as possible—formal and informal. (3) Give every task your best—even the odious ones. (4) Don't cry over spilt milk. Accept it—learn from it and go forward."

—*Vaughn LeRoy Beals, Jr., President*
Harley Davidson Inc.
Wisconsin

T_o be warm to people."

—*Gregory Hines, dancer and actor*
New York

❧

G_{ood} things and bad things come together—plunge in when you're ahead and fold when you're losing."

—*William S. Burroughs, author and artist*
New York

❧

H_{ealth} is more important than wealth. A harmonious marriage is better than the richest dowry. A genuine calling ranks above the loftiest office. Dedication to work is more rewarding than a high salary. A simple lifestyle is worth more than the greatest luxury. Contemplation and meditation have a better yield than restless diversion. Tranquillity of mind is a safer guarantor of peace than the strongest international accord. A happy home, good health, and a fulfilling profession—I consider these the greatest rewards one can expect in this world. To be cheerful one may also need the humility to believe in a higher creative force, the wisdom to accept the inevitable, the confidence to trust one's own judgment, and the luck to have another person in whom to confide."

—*Richard Mattessich, professor of accounting*
Faculty of Commerce & Business Administration
University of British Columbia
Canada

A healthy degree of self-confidence is key to leading a rewarding life."

> —*William Beslow, Matrimonial Attorney*
> *New York*

Family first."

> —*Graydon Carter, Editor*
> *Vanity Fair*
> *New York*

Find a job that you like and you will never work a day in your life."

> —*Clement Greenberg, art critic and author*
> *New York*

I think that there is a line that begins before our life here, intersects it, and continues after we exist. Chance certainly plays a part in our lives, but it is chance with a purpose."

—*Seiji Ozawa, Conductor and Music Director*
Boston Symphony Orchestra
Boston

The most important thing that I have learned early in life is to know God loves me and to love others as He loves me."

—*Mother Teresa*
Calcutta